Hello and welcome Let's Master British _.ung & Colloquialisms! If you're learning English as a second language, or perhaps wanting to improve your British dialect, this book is a great addition to harness your language skill set.

British Slang & Colloquialisms

Slang, no matter the language, is usually derived in order to establish individuality. Slang is often a very simple way to distinguish between native and non-native speakers. This is especially true for non-native English speakers; since English is a first language across many different countries and cultures, colloquial terms will differ quite dramatically.

In this book, we're going to focus on some of the most common colloquial terms and slang used in British English to help you adopt a native approach to your speech. Let's take a look at some popular words and phrases used today…

1. All bark and no bite

To say someone is all bark and no bite, we mean that they may be threatening to do something but they are actually unwilling to do it. You'll often hear someone referred to as "full of it" in this circumstance, too. "The teacher said he will suspend me if I don't finish this essay by tomorrow!"
"I wouldn't worry about Mr Baxter; he's all bark and no bite"

"Mandy gets so angry"
"I know what you mean, but she's all bark and no bite, she'd never actually do anything"

2. Barking mad
Off your head
Lost the plot
Nuts
A nutter

There are quite a few idiomatic phrases which have the same meaning in principle - referring to someone as being mad or crazy! Other common slang terms are "Mad as a box of frogs" and "Mad as a hatter" which derives from the Alice in Wonderland character The Mad Hatter!

You can use "barking mad", "off your head", "a nutter" and "nuts" and adjectives and adjectival phrases. This means you can just call people any of these words or phrases:

"You are absolutely barking mad,"

"You're a nutter but I love you,"

"Mary is barking mad, she just told me she can talk to cats!"

"Is he off his head? He definitely can't beat me in a race"

"Lost the plot" is a past tense phrase, so you use it with the verb "have"
"Have you lost the plot? We don't have that much money!"
"I think I've actually lost the plot"
"They have lost the plot"

Finally, you can use "nuts" with the verb "to go" to say that somebody became angry.

"She went nuts when I told her how much it cost!"

"To go nuts" can also mean to spend too much or to go over the top

"I promise I won't go nuts, but I do need quite a few things"
"Don't go nuts with baking cakes, there are only three of us"

3. Blooming

Blooming is used as an intensifier for sentences, for example "That was blooming lovely" or "I blooming hope not!". It has no real meaning other than to intensify your speech or to express surprise, for example in "Bloomin' hell!" or Bloomin' Eck!". Note that when we use the word "Blooming" to express surprise, we usually drop the -g for emphasis.

4. Chav

The word "Chav" became popular in the early 2000s in the UK, it's use became so widespread that it was even added to the Oxford English Dictionary. It's used as an insult, as it refers to someone as being antisocial and wearing cheap sportswear. It can also be used as an adjective, and you'll often hear the words "Chavvy" or "Chavvish" used to insult someone or something.
"You're such a chav, Julia!"
"That coat looks a bit chavvish"

5. Chinwag

This is a light-hearted term meaning to have a conversation or chat with someone. For example "It will be nice to catch up and have a chinwag over lunch".
It is basically a description of how your chin moves around or "wags" when you talk.
"It's about time we got together for a good old chinwag"
We can also use the word "Natter" as an alternative to chinwag… "We had a good old natter over a drink".

6. Copper

The term copper (or cop), refers to a police officer, and was originally thought to have derived from the copper buttons policemen wore on their uniforms. However, there are a couple of arguments over the term's origin; either a slang use of the acronym C.O.P (Constables on Patrol) or stemming from the verb "to cop" meaning to capture or to lay hold of something.

Here are some more police related terms:
"Bobby"; Used to describe a police officer and originating from the founder of the Metropolitan Police Sir Robert Peel (with Bobby being a nickname for Robert).
'boys in blue" - Another phrase which can be used to describe a police officer in reference to the blue uniform worn.

"Blues & Twos" - Blues & twos is a brilliant slang term referring to the flashing blue lights and sirens on a police car. You'll often hear it used as a noun in phrases such as "Here comes the blues and twos" and, confusingly, it can be used to refer to any emergency vehicles such as ambulances and fire engines even though the lights are no longer necessarily blue!

Finally, the terms "The Nick", "Cop shop" and "The Old Bill" are all slang for a police station.

7. Earwig / Nosy -

These terms are quite closely related to each other. To earwig means to listen in on someone's conversations whereas to be nosy usually means to pry into other people's affairs. Interestingly, nosy can be used as both an adjective (as in… "The nos neighbours") or a verb (Such as… "Stop being so nosy!")

8. Fiver / Tenner / Quid -

These are all slang words for different values of money in the United Kingdom, with a "quid" referring to a pound coin.

There are also some terms that are less than self-explanatory!

"Grand" - Meaning £1000 sterling

"Shrapnel" - Loose change

"Bronze" - Refers to the £1 and £2 coins

"Century" - Used in slang for £100 sterling

There are many slang words used as general terms for money, too. Here's some of the more common ones you may come across: "wod", "cheddar", "paper", "dough", "bread" and "dish".

9. Gaffer -

This is an informal way of describing one's boss or employer, thought to have distinguished from the 16th century, where a "gaffer" was the term used to describe the head of a group of labourers.
"I was ten minutes late this morning but don't tell the gaffer."

10. Geezer -

Geezer is a way to describe a man, particularly an old man. Whilst it's a very well-known slang term across the UK, it was traditionally an East London term; commonly known as cockney English! We'll explore more cockney terms later in this book.

11. Git -

Git is used as an insult to cite someone as being annoying or silly. It's common to use the word "prat" in a similar context, too, and both words are usually used in a harmless or joking fashion over implying anything nasty.

"Joe was being such a little git last night!"

"Don't be a prat, you need to calm down."

12. Grass / Snitch -

An informant, used to describe a person who has passed on confidential information about you. For example:

'He's grassed me up to the boys in blue"

'Jamie snitched on Michael for turning up to work late"

We often use the phrase "done the dirty" which has similar connotations. For example

He's done the dirty on me there!"

13. Jack the lad -

Someone who is a "Jack the lad" usually has the attributes of being cocky or brash.

14. Knackered / Shattered -

These are both synonyms for being tired and exhausted. There are quite a few more slang terms for being tired, including "spent", "beat" and "zonked".

15. Miffed -

Being miffed means to be slightly annoyed or offended by something (or someone).
"I was a bit miffed when they accused me of being late; I'm always on time."

16. Muck about -

The word Muck can be used in two completely juxtaposing slang phrases: To Muck About, and to Muck In

Mucking about refers to someone messing around or being silly.

"Quit mucking about and come help me."

"It was an easy day at work, all we did was muck about."

In contrary, to muck in with something means to help out and lend a hand to someone.

"We'll get the job done much quicker if we all muck in."

17. Mug -

Mug is used as a noun, describing someone as being gullible or easily-cheated. You'll often hear the phrases "I'm being taken for a mug" and "To mug someone off" which both have similar connotations, ie. to sell someone short.

18. Naff -

Used as an adjective, the word Naff describes something as lacking taste or style.
"The music was a bit naff so we left the party early."
Somewhat confusingly, the phrase "Naff all…" is also fairly common and means "nothing". For example:
"I went shopping yesterday but I got absolutely naff all."
"There was naff all left when I went to get something from the buffet."

19. Pig's Ear -

To make a pig's ear of something means to mess something up, or cause a problem.
"I tried to help but I made a right pig's ear of it".

20. Porkies -

"If someone accuses you of telling porkies, it means they think you're telling lies! It's usually used in jest or in a light-hearted situation.
Have you been telling porkies?"

21. See a man about a dog -

"This is a great euphemism, meaning to have a secret meeting or discussion. One of it's great uses is to subtly inform someone that they should mind their business and not pry!
What are you up to at the weekend?"
Going to see a man about a dog, how about you?"

22. The Tube -

The Tube is a widely adopted nickname for The London Underground; the underground railway system for London.

23. Wind up -

To wind someone up is an informal way to express teasing or joking with someone. "Having you on" is a similar slang term, too "He's only having you on."
"Don't wind your sister up, she's in a bad mood."

24. Skint -

Describing oneself as skint means to be short of or have no money.
"I'd love to come on holiday but I am too skint."

25. Cheeky -

Cheeky' has long been used in the UK to describe something light-hearted but a little rude or risqué. However, it is now used to describe any activity that is a little bit naughty but nice.
"Do you fancy a cheeky pint?"

26. Wasted -

Getting "wasted" is slang for becoming drunk or inebriated. There are so many more slang words we use for describing being drunk, not limited to: "Legless", "Sozzled", "Steaming", "Trashed", "Wrecked", "Hammered", "Sloshed","Bladdered" and "Drunk as a skunk". It's a long-standing joke in the UK that we can use any noun, adding "-ed" to the end to make a slang word for being drunk!
Cabbaged
Stewed
Zombied
Tanked
Even Goosed would work!
For a bit of fun, why not give it a go yourself?

Regional Differences

Despite its size, the UK is very dynamic with slang and colloquial expressions. It's quite common for some slang words or phrases to be localised to certain regions and areas, for example the South of England will often struggle to interpret a lot of the common sayings heard in the North. This usually results in a lot of topical debates!

One such hot topic is bread rolls… their naming differs hugely across the UK depending on your dialect, and you can often be met with a confused face in a restaurant if you order with the wrong one.

Some of the more common names are:
Bap
Barm - Which is local to Manchester in England
Breadcake
Bun - Which is popular in the north East of England
Cob - Which is common in the Midlands
Roll

There are many more, too! If you'd like some lighthearted entertainment it's certainly worth searching the internet for, you'll more than likely come across a heated debate on the matter! If you're curious, I personally use "Cob" as I'm based in the Midlands.

Let's explore some more regional differences…

1. **Remote control -** Colloquial terms for the remote control differ quite considerably between households rather than regions and include:

Doofer
Zapper
Clicker
Buttons
Switcher
Gizmo
Changer
Flipper
The Controls
The Wand

2. Mardy -

Mardy is a term local to the Midlands in England. It's used to describe someone as being grumpy or sulky.
We can also use the phrases:
"Having a paddy" or "Have a cob on" too - Not to be mistaken with the bread roll variety of course!
"Alex had a real cob on today so I told her to stop being mardy and join in with the game."

3. Being drunk

We explored the different words for being inebriated in the last section, and though a lot f those terms are universally understood, the majority have derived from different regions of the UK originally!
So whilst in Scotland you may hear people talking about getting Gatted or Goosed, you'll be getting Lashed in Manchester, Ankled in Bristol and Smashed in the South East!

4. Terms of endearment also differ regionally and are quite diverse!

- **"Love"** - Love is pretty universal in use, but originally comes from the North of England.   Word to the wise… whilst it is considered a term of endearment, some people view being called "love" as a little insulting and you can often be met with a vacant stare! —- "Do you need a hand, love?"
- **"Sug"** - Short for Sugar, this is common to the Midlands area, particularly in Stoke on Trent.   — "I'm ok for a drink, thanks, sug"
- **"Duck"** - This term again originated from the Midlands, more specifically from Derbyshire. In case you're wondering, this is my go-to term of endearment! — "Do you want a drink, duck?"

"My lover" - My lover is a brilliant greeting commonly used in the South West of England. It can be used as a greeting for strangers, friends and family, so don't panic if you hear someone calling you their lover - They don't mean it literally!!
"Alright my lover, how are you?"

"Babes" - If you're in Essex which is in the southeast of England, you'll hear this at the end of sentences all the time! It's a term which was adopted in the early noughties and used particularly by women "Babes, could you pick me up a sandwich?"

"Dear" - This is a very old term of endearment, dating back to around the early 14th Century and today, whilst the term is heard across the UK, it is typically used by older couples — not young people as much "Can I get you a drink, dear?"

"Pet" - Calling someone pet doesn't mean you think they're your little lapdog, it's a typical way to end a greeting to someone in the North East of England — "How are you, pet?"

"Hen" - It seems us Brits are quite fond of the animal terms! Hen is a term used for women across Scotland. "Do you need a bag for that, hen?"

5. Evening meal - Another controversial topic in the UK! An evening meal can be described as dinner, tea or supper depending on the region you live in. Whilst "dinner" is widely accepted, "tea" and "supper" derive from the North of the UK and can often confuse if used in the South! "What would you like for your tea tonight" "Are you stopping for supper?"

Rhyming Slang

Rhyming slang originates from the East End of London and is often regarded as "Cockney Rhyming Slang". It was originally developed as a way of obscuring the meaning of sentences to those who did not understand the slang, and is constructed by replacing the word with a phrase which rhymes - for example "Believe" becomes "Adam and Eve" as the last word rhymes to the original. "Can you Adam and Eve it?" The obscurity comes in force when the second word (the one that rhymes) is dropped from speech.

"Can you Adam it?"

Rhyming slang is very tricky to understand and whilst it's use is popular in the UK, it's certainly not hugely important for you to learn in order to sound more native. Having said that, it can be quite fun to learn the more popular expressions, so let's have a look at some…

1. Apples & Pears - Stairs
"Up the apples and turn left"

2. China Plate - Mate
"Are you alright me old China?"

3. Dog & Bone - Telephone
"Pass us the dog & bone, I'm going to give
them a bell"

4. Trouble & Strife - Wife
"I've been out all day with the trouble & strife"

5. Jam jar - Car
"Where's your jam jar today?"

6. Tomfoolery - Jewellery
"He brought her a nice of tomfoolery"

7. Ones and twos - Shoes
"Put your ones & twos on, we're going out"

8. Half-Inch - Pinch
"She had her phone half-inched"

9. Jack Jones - Alone
"Why are you sitting on your Jack Jones?"

10. Rabbit & pork - Talk
"Stop rabbiting on, we have stuff to do!"

Here are some more examples of Cockney rhyming slang. See if you can have a go at making up some sentences to use these in!

11. Loaf of bread - Head
12. Round the houses - Trousers
13. Ball and chalk - Walk
14. Lady Godiva - Fiver

Here are some of the words and phrases we've covered in this book. See how much slang you can remember!

1. Mardy - Moody
2. Skint - Having no money
3. Telling porkies - To tell lies
4. Doofer - Remote control
5. Bladdered - Drunk
6. Barm - Bread roll
7. Lost the plot! - Mad
8. Gaffer - Boss or person in charge
9. Chav - A derogatory term to insult someone as being "lower class"
10. Cob - Another term for a bread roll

So that's an introduction to British slang covered, I hope you've enjoyed the book! Languages are constantly evolving and slang is certainly no exception to this; with new words and phrases being introduced regularly, you can often find some terms very quickly become out of date. In this book we've covered some of the most common terms which have been carried through the decades.

Printed in Great Britain
by Amazon